This

The Adventures

of the Funny Bone

Joey Motes

The Adventures of the Funny Bone
© 2018 by Joey Motes

Published by Insight International, Inc.
contact@freshword.com
www.freshword.com
918-493-1718

All rights reserved. No part of this book may be reproduced or transmitted in any form or by any means, electronic or mechanical, including photocopying and recording, or by an information storage and retrieval system, without permission in writing from the author.

ISBN: 978-1-943361-50-2
Library of Congress Control Number: 2018932668

Printed in the United States of America.

DEDICATION

I dedicate this book to my grandson (Calvin Hudson, pictured on the back cover) and to my grandchild still in the oven. My desire for you is to live life to the fullest, knowing that you have a purpose. May you find in every adventure the meaning and the satisfaction. Leave your mark, make memories, and leave a trail through this life that others can follow. When there is pain, find the strength and fortitude to smile and laugh through it all.

CONTENTS

Foreword 7
Prologue 9
1. The Monster Snake Killing 11
2. The Man Had Lost His Wife 17
3. A Red Dot on a Plane 23
4. Only White Man in the Entire Country 29
5. Jumping over the Manhole 33
6. Go to Cedartown to See Eric 39
7. Wine Tasting on Communion Sunday 49
8. One Foot in the Grave 57
9. What's That Sound beneath My Feet 63
10. Meeting Mickey 69
11. Welcome to the Family 75
12. The Nap 81
13. I Don't Even Know That Man That Well 87
14. That's a Big Spider on the Wall 95
15. Red Meat in a Bag 101
16. Magic Mic 107

Foreword

I have had the pleasure of knowing Joey Motes for quite some time now. He was generous enough to grant me his daughter's hand in marriage, after an extensive Federal background check I'm sure. I liked him immediately. Truth be told, it's hard not to.

Joey has always had a knack for story-telling. His vibrant personality and abundance of wit is unmatched in my circle of friends and family. A room grows quickly quiet when Joey has the stage. It is not uncommon to see people leaning forward in their seats just to be closer to the action. Sometimes his stories are followed by a punch line, sometimes by a warm-hearted moral, and sometimes with a simple reminder that life is filled with both smiles and sniffles. But his stories are always followed with a "Got any more?"

Gathered in the pages of this book are true stories, told by the man himself—Joey Motes—in his own personal and special way. These stories are all factual retellings of actual events of Joey's life, connecting the reader to the author as the stories unfold.

The stories that follow are sure to tug on your heart strings...

...and definitely tickle your funny bone.

—Blake Hudson
Joey Motes' son-in-law

Prologue

When I was in middle school and high school, I was considered the class clown. In high school, I was voted "most school spirit". I don't believe that I received that award because I was a big supporter of our school mascot. I was awarded that title because I was so outgoing. In my adult life I have tried to live a Christian life style. In Christianity, the Good Book teaches us that we are the Body of Christ on the Earth. I think finding your place in life is one of life's precious questions. Where do I belong? How do I fit in?

When I speak in front of congregations across the nation, I am often introduced as the funny man—the preacher that makes you laugh. One of my friends recently told me, "Joey, when we are with you, we know we are going to laugh and we are going to get the Word." One of my friends in the ministry tells his congregation that when I speak, depression leaves the room. It is good to be known as someone who puts a smile on other people's faces. I don't try to be funny; it is not a planned out thing. I have accepted that humor is just in my makeup. Therefore, I tell people that I have found my place in the Body of Christ: "the funny bone".

The unique thing about the funny bone is that it is not a bone at all; it is a nerve in our elbow region. When we hit our funny bone, it sends a funny or numbing feeling through our arm. I think only the people who are not experiencing that weird feeling can call it funny. In *The Adventures of the Funny Bone,* I recall different situations that I have experienced in my life that have made me laugh and will hopefully put a smile on your face as well.

With each short story in this book, I try to share a life lesson. I am a firm believer that we can learn from every little thing we experience. In life, we can find ourselves in funny, lonely, painful, embarrassing, and hurtful situations. I think there are lessons we can learn in everyday life to pass along. It is my desire that you will be able to identify and connect with my humorous and painful findings presented through these stories.

In this book, I share lessons that I have learned that were very helpful to me. I hope that they will be helpful to you, too!

THE MONSTER SNAKE KILLING

I live on a dead end country road with only five houses on the street. We have only one street light on the entire road, and it is located at end of our driveway. Our house is the first house on the left. It's nice living on a street where the traffic is very limited and the timing of any vehicle is very predictable. It is also a very neighborly area. Our children can ride their bikes and their skate boards, and just walk down the half mile stretch of road without any worries.

When it comes to sleeping, I must have inherited my non-sleeping gene from my mother; she has never slept well. It is not uncommon for everyone in my house to sleep all night on any given night. As for myself—well let's just say my days are longer than most.

There was one particular night that I will never forget. The seasons were starting to change, the sweltering summer days and the hot summer nights were beginning to fade away. Warm days and cool nights had started; autumn was slipping in. On one of those nights that sleep had escaped me, I decided to go out for a walk on our street. The street light was shining and the moon was illuminating my surroundings. I could see very clearly, especially since I was very familiar with my neighborhood anyway.

I was in a very spiritual mood that night, and I was just so thankful for all that I had been blessed to obtain. I remember walking up and down our driveway, praying, and just being thankful for my wife and our child, our home, my health, a good job and good friends. You know, it is always good to stop, reflect, and count our blessings. After walking for a while, I decided to lie down on our dead end road. I just felt this super spiritual connection with my Creator. Simply put, it was awesome; I did not want it to end. The night air was brisk and the warmth of the asphalt was very inviting to me.

As I relaxed there on the road, all those spiritual emotions started to dissipate as my mind raced to an unforeseen but very possible problem. The warmth of the afternoon sun that the road had absorbed was being exhaled and the thought of those cold blooded reptiles coming to warm themselves for the night came to mind. We often see reptiles on the country roads that time of year warming themselves up for the cool night ahead. Why I had this thought in the middle of my spiritual time, Heaven only knows. Sure enough,

THE MONSTER SNAKE KILLING

I looked out of the corner of my eye, and there he was—laying there in the grass next to the road. The reflection of the street light combined with the moonlight gave me a mighty clear view of it. This snake was on his way to the pavement to get warm on this chilly night. Being the man of the house and the protector that I am, there would be no intruders into our neighborhood without a fight!

I had at the time what we country folks call a shed in my backyard. A shed is a covering for some of your most valuables, a covering to place all your stuff–or junk as some would say. Sheds can contain such items as old bikes, wood projects that had been started and never completed, push mowers, parts of other push mowers, rakes, shovels, hoes, other such tools, and the other varieties of valuable things that people put in sheds. Well, my thought was to retrieve my hoe from the shed and hurry back to the street before the old cold blooded intruder could slither away.

Did I fail to mention that I had no electrical lighting of any kind in that old shed? It must be Murphy's Law that the item you always need the most is behind all the other valuables in storage. That was the case this night. I climbed over and under stacked wood, moving this and dropping that until at last I had it. Never mind that I was not dressed properly to be climbing around and through a shed in the middle of the night; I knew I had to find that tool! I wasn't wearing any shoes, only a tee shirt and my fancy "I hope no company stops by" pajamas. Nevertheless, I was determined to protect my loved ones.

By this time my adrenaline was racing, and I was not at all concerned about getting bit by another possible snake in the shed or tripping over the tiller and breaking my neck. I was on a mission. My family was asleep safe and sound in the house and I was going to keep it that way.

As fortune would have it, when I returned, the snake was still laying there in the same spot. It was a cool night and snakes don't like moving fast when it is cool. I made my way into hoe reach (it's like arm's reach, but for when you're holding a hoe). Bare feet, pajamas and all, I took care of business. All was safe and order had been restored to our community.

Needless to say, there was no going to bed and getting any amount of sleep to speak of after that excitement. After laying down and waking around 5:00 to head to work, I couldn't wait to tell my co-workers about the snake I had killed. I guess like any other man, my snake story became the fish tale of the day. My little snake turned into an anaconda by the end of my shift. By the time I recounted the story over and over, the bed of my truck was not big enough to carry the poor little dead thing around.

This was before the age of cell phones, so I hadn't spoken to my wife and daughter about my heroics all day. I raced home after work to tell them

The Monster Snake Killing

about the event. When I got home, the conversation started with a big soft welcome home kiss, and then my story began.

"Hey honey, let me tell you what happened last night while you were sound asleep. I was outside praying and a snake came up and I killed it," I said to my wife with a smile.

My wife responded, "Another snake!"

I stopped for a moment, looking puzzled. "Another snake? What do you mean?"

She told me that my daughter and some friends were playing outside and the boys had killed a snake yesterday.

Yes, I killed a dead snake! The boys down the road had killed the little fellow and I had re-killed it!

You know that is the way many of us live our lives. We are still fighting and afraid of something that has already been defeated. I know the devil roams around roaring like a lion, but he is no lion. All he can do is make noise. When Jesus went to Calvary, He conquered everything that old slue foot had to offer. The Victory has been won. We are on the winning side and Jesus is the Lion of the tribe of Judah, the King, the Victor!

> *Stop beating on a dead enemy and live your life as a victor and not a victim.*

Stop beating on a dead enemy and live your life as a victor and not a victim. Whom shall I fear with all that Jesus has conquered for us?

On the highway of life, there is rest and peace for everyone. We do not have to continue to risk our lives in the shades of our past, climbing over all the obstacles that could have destroyed us. Wake up and see that the enemy is defeated and Christ has conquered all!

THE MAN HAD LOST HIS WIFE

I slowly pull into the driveway of this traditional brick ranch home that I had never seen before, not knowing exactly why I was doing it.

I had purchased my first home about ten miles outside the limits of our city. Being new to the area, there are many things that one had to learn to function properly: where to pay local utilities, the best convenience stores, and where to take your weekly trash. It is amazing how much garbage a family can create in a week's time. In the city, one can have their trash picked up for a small fee. Out in the country, there are locations where big blue dumpsters are placed where you can just pull up and unload your car or take the trash out of the back of your pick truck up and throw it in the dumpster.

Being new to the area, I wasn't positive of the nearest location of a trash dumpster. I had asked a man at a local store and he pointed me in the right direction to take care of my weekly trash business.

I remember it like it was yesterday. I was driving down a very narrowly paved road—very unfamiliar to me. As I recall, it was my first time ever being on that old country road. This part is difficult to explain; I was driving and this brick home just jumped out at me. I can almost say it was on the road in front of me. It was so weird! It sounds strange I know, but I don't have any other way to describe it. I can't say looking back that I just dismissed the peculiarity of it, but nevertheless I did continue to drive on until I located the big dumpster.

After unloading my pickup truck load of trash, I drove back down the road that I had driven in on. As I approached the brick home that had jumped out at me on the way to find the dumpster, I slowly pulled into the driveway. At the time it was like an outer body experience. I did not have any expectations; I just knew I had to turn in. What was to take place after that...well I still did not know. Looking back, I cannot tell you whether I turned into the driveway or whether a higher power had guided the steering wheel. Whatever got me there, I was there.

I opened the door of my truck and made my way to the side door under the house's carport. On most ranch style homes, there is a front door and a side door located under a carport. We country folks mainly

The Man Had Lost His Wife

use the carport door, so that's where I went. I definitely didn't know why I was knocking on the carport door of the house that I had never even seen before, and I wasn't sure if I had even started or finished knocking when some very crucial thoughts entered my mind. What was I going to say when the door opened? Was I asking for directions? How was I going to explain how I got there?

I am a believer of the Creator of the universe, and I know that He knows all things and cares about everything concerning our lives. When we meet people who feel the same way, it gives us believers a peace that is difficult to explain. As the carport door opened, there I stood with this older gentleman in his late seventies or possibly his eighties standing in front of me. I don't remember what happened next or exactly how it happened, but this older gentleman had walked out of his home and had placed his arms around me and was crying.

Yes, I was at a strange person's home in a strange area with a strange older gentleman's arms around me. He was crying and I was just assuring him it was going to be alright. I did not even know where I was or who I was encouraging. I am not even sure how long we embraced. It could have been minutes and it could have been over a half hour. I was there and it was a God thing.

> *I was there and it was a God thing.*

Right there on that country road, in an area that I had never been to before, was a man inside his ranch style home grieving. His long time love of over forty years had passed away three months prior to me showing up on his doorstep. I know how these things work, so I talked about how difficult it is when a loved one passes away. In the unforeseen or even the expected end of a loved one, there are so many supporters and family members and neighbors to help love and care for the survivors. We all mean well when we tell those we love, "If you need me, just call." I truly think that when others tell their loved ones that, they mean it.

Three months had passed. All of the flowers had faded and all the cards were just a reminder. All of the food that neighbors had brought was gone, all of his family and friends were back to their routine lives, but his life would never be back to routine without his sweetheart. A man in his home, lonely and broken hearted, was facing reality…she was gone!

Did I have magic words? Did I have an embrace that no one else could offer? After all, I did not even know this man or his situation. Simply put, I was at the right place at the right time, and I was willing. I was willing to just believe, willing to be used for the greater good, and willing to be wherever and do whatever the guiding of my Lord led me to do. Have I ever missed it? Oh Yes! But this day, I believe the Lord used me to comfort a man who was in his home alone and grieving.

The only one who knew the heart and the pain of this man was the One who caused a little brick home to jump out at a man only wanting to get rid of his trash. I am so glad we have a God who knows all our cares!

> *Did I have magic words? Did I have an embrace that no one else could offer?*

There are two things I'd like to share with you. First, be encouraged today. The Lord knows and cares about every fiber of your being. He cares for your health, He cares for your family, He cares for your finances, and He cares for your total wellbeing. No matter what you face in this life, know that the Lord cares for you. Secondly, I tell myself and others to be alert on how the Spirit can speak to you at any time and in any situation. Be ready at any given moment. You may be the person who sees a home jump out at you, or you could be the person inside the home.

A RED DOT ON A PLANE

Our church has been involved with a ministry in Zambia for many years now. I have a good friend named Bishop Joseph S. Kazhila who lives in Zambia and heads up a Christian school in a very rural area. Every time I visit, I leave with so much appreciation for all the blessings we have in America. I know, like most of you know, that the television commercials about orphans and hungry children in all parts of the world are real. What we are most skeptical about is if we send money, how much will the children actually receive? Years ago, I met Bishop Kazhila in a conference in Atlanta that a church had sponsored for him to attend. We hit it off and remained in touch through letters. Bishop Joseph asked me if I could come to Zambia. I agreed to visit him, and we have had a spiritual connection ever since.

I have traveled to Zambia on several occasions. It is a long, hard trip. I usually leave Atlanta, Georgia and travel to Gatwick, London—which takes approximately eight and half hours. In Gatwick, I may have a layover of eight to twelve hours. The connecting flight from London to South Africa can take over eleven hours. I have been very fortunate that most connecting flights from Johannesburg to Zambia average three to five hours. Needless to say, one can be pretty tired and worn out after making this trip. On one occasion, I was flying from London to Johannesburg, South Africa and I found myself seated by a woman with a red dot on her forehead.

The international flights are made on huge airplanes. This particular flight was on a 747 British Airway plane. As I made my way down the aisle checking for my seat number, I noticed someone in my seat. These planes are massive and yet every seat is usually taken. I always ask for an aisle seat. A window seat is acceptable, but when I am flying long distances I hate being trapped in a row. The seat by the window offers great views and even a place to lay your head. However, the window seat has more disadvantages than advantages for someone like me. I need to move around. I have to stretch and walk around. If I sit by the window and have to get up and walk around, I would have to disturb people who may be sleeping. I guess I have a touch of claustrophobia. On each side of the plane there are usually three seats with a row in the middle for about five passengers. I have found it is much more convenient for me and everyone around me if I have the aisle seat.

So I finally found my aisle seat that I so greatly desired, and there was a woman sitting in it. We checked our tickets and this lady and her mother sitting beside her each simply needed to shift one seat over to make room for me and give me my precious aisle seat. We placed our carry-on bags overhead and settled in for the departure. As we taxied out onto the runway, I noticed that this lady and her mother pulled out a statue and began to move their lips. I definitely thought they were praying. You can ask anyone—I do not meet strangers and I have no problem striking up a conversation. Since I have been somewhat of a world traveler, my curiosity of other cultures and customs is really pronounced. I am very inquisitive, and inquiring minds want to know! So, I asked the two women what they were just doing. The lady who spoke good English said, "We were praying."

"Oh, ok! I was just wondering." I replied. "So you won't be offended if I pray as well?" She said of course not, so I prayed to my God. I do not know if her religion teaches that her relic can hear or even help any request. I am thankful to pray to a God who hears me.

After settling in for the flight, we started to talk. The younger woman's name was Deepa. I cannot recall her mother's name. She told me that they had been on vacation in Europe and were headed home. They lived in South Africa. After sharing several things about where they had traveled to on this vacation, we spoke about our personal lives. I told her about myself, about how I was married and had one child. She told me that she was married but had no children. I asked what the red dot on her forehead was for. She said it was like my wedding ring; it was a sign that she was married. I had assumed it was some religious symbol or sign of some religious system.

We flew for what seemed like days. On these long flights they serve you several meals. After eating, there isn't much to do, so most people typically go to sleep. As Deepa slept, she tossed and turned trying to get comfortable. She must have slept two or three hours. It was about an hour and a half before landing when the stewardess came around to serve the final meal. People on the plane started to rouse about and wake up. I looked over at Deepa, who at one point was sleeping with her head almost on my shoulder. As she awakened, we did not speak but I noticed her red dot was gone off of her forehead. It was on my shoulder!

"Deepa, what does this mean?" I asked with a grin. We both just laughed and said that it means it must be a long flight. This woman had a great personality.

Sometimes in life we take ourselves too seriously. Life is too short. Loosen up. Stop and smell the roses.

A Red Dot on a Plane

Notice the red dots. Enjoy the moments. I am so thankful that she had a good sense of humor. Not everyone you meet can just laugh things off.

> *Sometimes in life we take ourselves too seriously.*

I conduct many weddings. I always meet with the bride and groom and each time we meet I try to put into perspective their big wedding day. I tell them to slow down, embrace everything, and take it all in. Some brides fail to even see the flowers they spent months picking out. They don't take a glance at the guests they invited or even notice their own bridal party. They become consumed with the big event and miss it while being there. I don't want to miss anything. I want to embrace life with humor and adventure.

All of us can travel through life and experience restlessness and new adventures. It is best not to get heated when someone is in your seat. You never know, the stranger you are beside could send you her dot!

ONLY WHITE MAN IN THE ENTIRE COUNTRY

It's safe to assume that you are already having thoughts race through your mind about the title to this chapter. As I have stated previously, I travel to many places outside of my own country. On this particular trip I was in Zambia for my first visit. My friend and ministry son, Bishop Joseph Kazhila, was hosting me. On this day, he needed a part for his vehicle. In the area where we were, there were no parts stores like we have in the United States.

We went to this huge open market which resembled a city wide flea market. You could purchase about anything at this place. People had most anything and everything for sale or trade: rugs, chairs, baskets, quilts, fish, vegetables, fruits, sugar, and even medicines. Yes, there were car parts there as well. It was simply amazing to me to observe Joseph as he made his way through the hundreds and thousands of people asking in his native language where to find the part he needed. I remember it was a water pump for his truck that he was in need of. I must tell you that of all the items there for sale or trade, I would not be afraid to say that ninety-nine percent of those items were used and used to the max.

It was a great experience to see how the natives did everyday business and conducted their lives. I have always been intrigued by other cultures. On this day, I could not understand their communication or any other facet of their business dealings. If you have ever been in a situation like that, one of not knowing the language and not having a firm understanding of the currency, it can bring real fear and confusion. When a group of people are speaking in a language that I have never even heard before, I always assume they are speaking about me, and probably not about me in a good way. When there is an exchange of money and I don't know the breakdown of the exchange rate, I always feel like I am getting ripped off.

On this particular day, I was standing and taking in all the sounds and the sites around me. As far as I could see, Zambian people were everywhere. All of a sudden, it occurred to me that I was maybe the only white man in this entire country. Now I know that my thought wasn't true, but from my perspective it sure resembled being true. Over that entire countryside, over each little valley and over each little horizon, there were Zambians everywhere. After all, I was in Zambia! I thought to myself, "I must really stick out like a sore thumb."

Then something happened. About two hundred yards away, through hundreds of people, I saw them. All of a sudden, the Zambian people moved back and allowed for a clear view. It was like the parting of the Red Sea. There were two white people standing in the distance. It was like one of those romantic television commercials: our eyes met, we shared a look, and then music started playing. I started making my way toward them and they started in my direction. It was in slow motion as I recall. We turned left then right, dipped here then there, all in an attempt to avoid the crowd until we reached each other.

"Hello!" I said with excitement as I vigorously shook the man's hand.

They replied, "Jshoiuhdiouhihdsh." I had no clue what they were saying. They may not have been from Zambia, but they sure enough weren't from my home town. I could communicate with the Zambians better than I could with these two. It's really funny now, but boy it sure was a letdown at the time.

How many times do we experience these same emotions when we are in very unfamiliar settings? Many times we are made to feel like we must be the only ones experiencing this kind of life. I read about a man in the Good Book that was dealing with these same issues. Elisha had just had a great victory, and he was running and was fearful for his life. He sat down and bowed his head. Elisha prayed, "I am the only prophet left Lord. Take my life before they kill me."

God had to remind Elisha that he was not the only prophet left, and that He had seven thousand more prophets. When we start feeling isolated and all alone, those emotions are used against us. I am confident that I am never alone in my lonely times. I decided years ago to believe. My belief is that I have angels with me. The Bible says that they that are with me are greater than they that are against me. I believe that the Lord is ever present with me.

You may be in a distant country, or you may be in your own home, but the enemy can make you feel like you are the only one dealing with what you are facing. The enemy is a liar. One of the reasons that Jesus came was to experience the very emotions and pains and loneliness we experience. Our Heavenly Father knows everything you are dealing with; you are not alone!

> *I believe it was just God's way of saying that I wasn't there by myself.*

Even though I could not communicate with that couple, it sure did me a lot of good by just seeing them and feeling their hug and handshake. I believe it was just God's way of saying that I wasn't there by myself.

Jumping over the Manhole

I have found that it is always good to have friends. Many people have acquaintances and social media friends. In this case, I am talking about those real friends—those people that you share your life with and have common interests with. In my early twenties, I was very close to two brothers. Gary and Cliff ran a store in our community and raced dirt bikes. I loved going to all the different towns to watch them race. I told myself that I was helping them out, but I was there just to cheer them on more than anything. I never raced and I just did not have a desire to get on a motocross bike and jump in the air. I had witnessed too many crashes, especially from Gary and Cliff. They did talk me into buying a bike one time, but I will refrain from telling that story here. Let me just say that I did not make it home with the bike from the dealership, and I ended up having to go into surgery to fix my mistake.

Every single week we would travel to some race in some old racing town. All week long, we would discuss what happened at the prior race while discussing the upcoming race. Those were the good ole days.

I think Cliff and his wife had a daughter already and I am positive that Gary and his wife had a young daughter. Gary and his wife Connie were expecting a baby boy. It just so happened that the baby arrived on a day when I was on jury duty.

Jury duty is a learning experience if you have never been selected. The process seems very slow and a waste of a whole lot of money, if you ask me. I have been on several trials as a juror over the years. The fascination about the judicial system is worn off of me. Don't get me wrong, I do appreciate our laws and court systems and I do think that it is our duty to do our part as a citizen. However, as a citizen, I see were some improvements could be made.

On this day, I was at the court house going through the process to be picked with a hundred other jurors for different cases. In the selection process, lawyers from both the prosecution and the defense ask potential jurors questions that could help their case. Since the "new" of being on a jury had worn off for me, I was just fine with being dismissed as not chosen as a juror.

I have tried everything over the years to not get chosen as a juror. I have spoken up and told them that I was whole-heartedly for the death penalty. They still chose me. I have said that I am very much against the death penalty. They still chose me. I have said that I know the defendant and I'm related to the lawyer. They still chose me. It is what it is.

I had gotten word that Gary and Connie had a brand new baby boy. When the court went into recess for an hour and half at lunch, I had plenty of time to leave the court house and go by and offer my congratulations to the new parents. Wouldn't you know it—it was raining harder that I can remember ever seeing it rain. I was dressed really nice that day. When you go to the court house, one needs to present himself well and dress in nice clothes. I did not have a suit or tie on but I did have on my best dress pants with a nice button up shirt along with my Sunday "go to meeting" penny loafers. Those shoes are real stiff because you only wear them to special events like going to church or serving at the court house.

When we were given our lunch break at the court house, I decided to go to the hospital and see my friend. I just could not find a parking space anywhere close to the entrance of the hospital. I had to drive across the street from the hospital to find a park. As I got out and started running up the street towards the hospital entrance I couldn't help but notice that it was raining harder. Like the average male, I had no umbrella. As a result of that day, however, I do carry one today.

I looked up ahead in the street and I could see some construction workers scurrying about trying to finish whatever they were working on. I saw the orange cones, the big orange traffic signs, and the big equipment they had been using to dig up the road. I saw the cement truck sitting to the side, still turning the fresh cement. I even saw the big piece of steel in the road that they use to cover a hole after they finish their work. What I did not see was that the big piece of steel was not over the hole, it was beside the hole. In the open hole was freshly poured cement.

I can still see it in my mind's eye. I was running through the rain while those construction guys were minding their own business and working. Then I saw that rain-soaked steel lying in the road. My mind told me that those penny loafers hitting that wet steel plate would cause me to slip and fall. I did not want to slip and fall, get soaking wet, and get embarrassed right in front of those construction worker guys. So while running at full speed, I made the decision to jump.

If that steel plate had been over that hole, there would be nothing to tell today. After I jumped, right in front of God and all those people, I landed in the freshly poured concrete that came up clear to my knees.

I didn't see the look on those men's faces, but I bet they still talk about the day when this crazy, soaking wet man ran and jumped right in the middle of their concrete. Thank God they had a water hose there to help rinse off some of the concrete and mud. I did what I could with the water they supplied, but it did very little to help me look presentable for the hospital visit or back at the court room. Needless to say, I did not to congratulate my friends or see their new baby. I had to hurry home and change clothes to make it back to jury duty. Thank goodness for long lunch breaks.

There is more than a few times in life when things don't go as planned. You have to learn to go with the flow. We have to take some things with a grain of salt. It is much better not to take everything so seriously. I have always been able to laugh at myself. Believe me, I give myself plenty to laugh at.

> *You have to learn to go with the flow.*

People that are uptight or on edge are folks that I call "211 people." I say that because water boils at 212 degrees. Many people are just one degree from blowing their top; they are just one event from going off entirely. Today in our society, so many people are heated and ready to explode. Slow down, take it easy, and enjoy the small things. Take a walk, breathe the air, lie on your back in a field and take in the blue sky. Go for a run in the rain...just avoid the man holes!

GO TO CEDARTOWN TO SEE ERIC

Growing up in my family meant getting together at Thanksgiving and Christmas with aunts and uncles and cousins at my grandparents' house. My dad's family lived mostly in Alabama and we always drove to my maw maw and pawpaw's house for the holidays. My mother's family is mostly located in Georgia and close to where I grew up as a boy. My mom and dad both had six brothers and sisters each, and that made for plenty of cousins. Getting together for the holidays was more like controlled chaos. Christmas gatherings were always fun, and I still have so many memories from my childhood.

Recalling the times when we would go to Alabama for Thanksgiving and Christmas, a few things stand out to me. First of all, the food my maw maw would cook and how she would place a sheet over the food on the table. Most every house back then had a screen door that had at least two or three holes in it that made easy access for the flies to get in. Putting a sheet over the food made plenty of sense. If we were lucky, maw maw would have one of those sticky tape things hanging from the ceiling right over the food table that would catch all the flies. It was not uncommon to walk into the house and see this twelve or fourteen inch sticky tape contraption hanging from the ceiling covered in flies that had become prey to its fatal trap.

I remember standing in front of the gas heater on extremely cold days and getting real hot on one side and real cold on the other side and then taking turns at the heater with another family member. We would also go outside and play football with all my cousins and uncles. It was so much fun. My dad would borrow a pair of his dad's overalls and hide the football inside the oversized clothes. It was our secret play that everyone knew about.

You did not want to miss Christmas time in Alabama as a kid. Each and every year, there would be more gifts than a person could count stacked around the tree. The gifts would be stacked up so high that you could hardly see the Christmas tree behind them. Wrapped gifts stacked taller than the Empire State Building was a definite "wow" for an eight to ten year old to see! We would tear through those gifts in mere minutes. When your name was called, your heart would begin to race. Your gift could be politely handed to you or thrown at you from across the room. We enjoyed socks, hats, chocolate covered cherries, or some type of ball or toy. Man, those were good times. The best part was that every item was either labeled with the Alabama or Auburn football team logo.

When we would get together with my mother's family in Georgia, we called it going to pawpaw and granny's. My pawpaw was a preacher, so the whole family would sit around and sing gospel songs around the piano after we ate. Pawpaw always played piano with his hands going way up in the air. You would have to see it for yourself to understand. My family and all those who knew Frank Sharp know what I am talking about.

As I mentioned earlier, we had a big family in Georgia as well as in Alabama. I remember eating with a broken fork that was a signature item at pawpaw and granny's house. It was supposed to have four prongs like a normal fork, but one was missing. Pawpaw said the fork lost one prong when he was extra hungry one day. I also remember that before we opened up any Christmas gifts we had to wait on everyone to finish eating. Can I tell you that those grownups were the slowest eating people in the world! You could bet on one thing, after they finished all of the Christmas food, they were going to sit around the table a drink coffee for what seemed like eight hours.

The kids would go outside to play tag or chase or something of that sort to pass the time. Pawpaw had these big silver leafed trees that he had painted white about four feet off the ground. Those trees always stood out to me because I do not remember ever seeing anyone else who had painted trees in their yard.

One of my cousins is named Eric. His dad is Gary, my mother's brother. Eric is about five years younger than me. Eric stood out as a young boy; he had very blonde hair. With our age difference, I wasn't very close to Eric. Like most other family members as children, we began to grow apart as we began to grow older. Years went by and I could not tell you the last time that I had seen Eric. Neither his schooling, nor his hobbies, nor anything else about Eric and his life were on my radar.

Before I started pastoring a church, I went to a church that taught about the power of the Holy Spirit. Carol and I learned a great deal about the spiritual aspects of living a life under the leadership of the Holy Spirit. We dedicated our lives to being faithful Christians.

My uncle Gary knew I was preaching and a regular church member when he saw me out in town one day. I do not remember where we met but I do remember Uncle Gary's request. He asked me if I would pray for his son Eric.

I didn't have to ask what was wrong—you can read between the lines when a parent is asking for prayer

Go to Cedartown to See Eric

for their child. Eric was not sick, nor did he need a job or any other financial help. He was involved with some bad people and some illegal activities that could lead to his arrest, or even the end of his life. I told my uncle that I would gladly pray for Eric.

I know that I am not much different from any other person. I left committing to praying for Eric, but after a few times of praying for him, I stopped. I didn't stop praying because I did not care or I felt like God was not hearing me, I stopped praying because I would just forget to do it.

Several months went by. Carol and I were at church on a Saturday afternoon with several other people praying about a host of issues. Our church, at the time, had women pray on one side of the church and men pray on the other side. I remember it now so clearly. As I was praying, I heard the Holy Spirit tell me to go to Cedartown and see Eric. It was so clear and persuading that I immediately got up from praying. I walked over to where my wife was praying and told her I was going to Cedartown to see Eric, so she would need to find herself a ride home.

Now, I do not remember driving the twenty mile trip. I did not entertain the notion of whether or not I would even get to see Eric, I just went. I do recall pondering on exactly what I would say to him if I did get the chance to see him. Would I say the wrong thing? Would I even know what to say? Then the

Scripture came to my mind, "Don't take thought what to say in that hour, for I will bring things to your remembrance of what to speak." With that, I had confidence that I would say the right thing.

As I drove into Cedartown, Georgia, I came to a hotel that was in the shape of an "L". The office came down and out away from the main portion of the hotel and the wing of the hotel where most of the rooms were located sat behind the office. There was something very strange about that day. When I drove into the parking lot of the hotel, not one single car was in the lot. It was about five o'clock in the evening and it was still daylight. I got out of the car and entered the office. No one was in the office. I rang the little silver bell located on the counter top. Still no one came. I found myself walking behind the counter and with a raised tone in my voice I asked if anyone was there. After a few tries, to no response, I made my way back to my car. When I got into my car, I noticed a door open to one of the rooms way down from the office. I don't know why but I found myself back in my car and driving toward that room.

As I drove up and parked just outside of that room, I noticed that the door and the window curtains were both open. I noticed that a man was vacuuming the room. My first instinct was not to surprise the person cleaning the room because he had his back to me. Instead of walking up on the room to announce my presence, I decided to blow my car's horn. This is when it all went according to plan. Well, not my plan—but His plan.

As soon as I blew the horn, the door of the hotel room next to the room where the man was cleaning opened. There stood a man who was over six feet tall, dressed in black, had a shaved head, and had tattoos around his neck. It was Eric.

Eric had ordered a pizza and thought that it had arrived when he heard the horn blow. He knew who I was and I knew that it was him. Not wanting to act surprised to see him, and having a very outgoing personality anyway, I just got out of my car and greeted Eric. We shared a very basic "Hello" and "How've you been" and then Eric asked me to come into his room. He was as surprised to see me as I was to see him. As I entered the room, there was neither alcohol nor drugs of any kind. There was a big pistol located on the night stand. Eric knew that I was a minister and I knew the life he was living. There was no need to speak of those things, so we spoke of our times as kids at pawpaw's house.

Eric had been staying with other people who lived an active drug life style. He told me he just needed a night away to relax. It is a life style where one has to stay on guard at all times because you never know when a friend could become an enemy. No one knew he was at that hotel and he knew there was no way that a cousin who he had not seen in years would know where he was.

If you are waiting for lightning bolts in this story, there were none. I stayed for a while. Eric ate pizza and drank soda and I ate with him. I did not stay a long time, because guys don't talk a lot in the first place. In this case, no words that I could have conjured up could even have come close to the real reason why I was there. I told Eric that if he ever needed me for anything, to not to hesitate to call. He said that he would.

> The real story is that the Lord knew exactly where he was.

You see, the real story here is not that I found my cousin Eric in a nearby town, the real story is that the Lord knew exactly where he was. There are so many people who feel lost in this life. Those people believe that no one knows how they feel and that no one knows where they are. People may not know, but the Lord Jesus knows.

That night in the hotel room, Eric did not confess to me that he wanted a change in his life. But, I believe that night did make an impact of my cousin. Not long after that, Eric made his way to a church service and asked God for help. Today, Eric works with the homeless in Florida. He is clean, sober, and has a wonderful family.

For people who want to escape their pain and who want to hide and run away from the troubles of this life, the world offers many options. The problem is that the world has many paths that will lead you down dark alleys that will lead you into a dark hole where you will find yourself trapped. The world is designed to make things heavy and difficult. We are no match for the world on our own. We are not created to handle all that life throws our way. One of the first things we find in the Good Book is the phrase, "It is not good for man to be alone."

When life is heavy and the load of everyday living weighs you down, Jesus told us to cast all of our cares upon Him. Eric and I always remembered a particular song pawpaw would play on the piano. The lyrics of this one song were, "If you move over just a little bit, I will help you carry your load."

I'm asking you, friends—don't do life alone. Connect with others. Connect with people who have faith, with people who can makes positive deposits into your life. Connect with people who encourage you and challenge you. Connect with Christian believers. Connect with people who are going somewhere in life. But most of all, connect with Jesus.

When we feel lost—and at times we all do—cry out of your soul and something amazing will happen. Our heavenly Father hears from heaven and He knows right where we are. Just ask the one sheep who got separated from the ninety nine, or ask the woman who lost one single coin and searched the house diligently until she found it. You are His child and He cares for you. He is not willing that anyone should be lost. He is searching for you.

WINE TASTING ON COMMUNION SUNDAY

Communion is one of those sacred observances in the Christian church. Each observance always stands out in my mind as a holy moment. Communion is derived from the Feast of Passover in the Bible, when Israel had been held captive by the Egyptians. Without going into great detail, it was the Israelites' last night in bondage and the death angel was going to come to every home. You were to have the blood of an innocent lamb applied to the door post of your home. When the death angel saw the lamb's blood, he would pass over that particular home. It was a great deliverance for the Israelites that night. From that time forward, the Israelites would observe Passover as a reminder of the great deliverance God had made for them.

In the time of Jesus, He and His disciples were observing the Passover feast when Jesus took a cup of wine, blessed it, drank it, and told his followers that the wine represented His blood—and the New Covenant of sacrifice. Jesus then took bread, blessed it, ate it, and told His followers that it represented His body. Jesus went on to say that this was of the New Covenant: that whoever ate and drank in His name would be showing reverence to the covenant. Jesus said, "As often as you do this, do it in remembrance of Me."

That is what we call communion in the Christian church. Communion is observed on special occasions throughout the year. Easter, Christmas, and New Years are some of the typical times for the observance of communion. In some settings, communion takes place as often as the leadership of the church deems necessary. That is where my story begins.

I had not been pastoring very long. My little flock was growing and we were having some very spiritual services. People were getting saved and their lives were being changed. People were receiving the baptism of the Holy Ghost. There were numerous testimonies of people getting healed; it was all very exciting. The worship music was always uplifting and charismatic. New people had started coming to the church. For this young minister, things were looking up.

One family of particular importance to this story is the Couey family, Frank and his wife Brenda. Now,

Wine Tasting on Communion Sunday

Brenda was called "Big Momma' by her friends. I never called her that; I chose to call her Mrs. Brenda. Frank and Brenda Couey were some of the best people you could ever meet. Frank was a hard worker and a good man. Mrs. Brenda was an excellent cook, thus the origin of her nickname. She was always cooking and having people over or going to someone's house with a spread of food impressive enough to feed a small army. I am proud to say that I ate Mrs. Brenda's cooking on many occasions. She is has since passed away, and I sure do miss her.

The Coueys had not been coming to my church more than three months when the incidents of this story took place. All of those Christian experiences were somewhat new to them. On a certain Sunday, I announced that the following Sunday we would be observing the Lord's Communion. Unlike most churches that I had been part of in my life, we used real unleavened bread and real wine. I would usually purchase a kosher wine, and I would ask someone in the church to make the unleavened bread—bread made without yeast. In the Bible, yeast is a symbol of sin. When Jesus said to take and eat of His body, His body was without sin. This is why we observe Communion with bread with no yeast: to remind us that Jesus was the Lamb who was innocent and free from sin. The wine represents the blood that was applied to the door posts that saved the Israelites and saves us when we have the blood of Jesus applied to our lives.

After I announced that the following Sunday we would be observing communion, Mrs. Brenda came to me and said, "Pastor Joey, we have some homemade wine, and I want to get rid of it. Could I bring it for the communion service?" Being a novice in the wine market and definitely knowing absolutely nothing about homemade wine, I said yes.

The following Sunday we were ready for a solemn communion ceremony. The congregation turned out in great numbers. The songs were planned and played with perfection. The table was set with a clean, white table cloth with the communion serving dishes placed on top of it. The communion bread was placed in a golden serving dish. The communion wine was ready to be served out of a golden serving tray. Each serving dish had been polished and was shining like a star for this special moment.

When communion is observed, each church member gets a piece of unleavened bread, scripture is read, and a prayer is prayed. Each member then eats the bread in remembrance of the Lord's body that was given as a sacrifice for all believers. Next, each person is given a small communion cup of wine. Scripture is read and a prayer is prayed. The wine symbolizes the He shed blood of Jesus. After everyone drinks the wine, a song is sung.

Wine Tasting on Communion Sunday

This day was different, however. The mood was solemn and everything was in order. The deacons were in their proper place, the Lord's Table was front and center, and the proper décor outlined the table elegantly. The lights were properly set; they were not too bright and not too dim. Soft instrumental music played in the background to help cement the solemnity of the occasion. The Scriptures were marked for the proper readings. The communion dishes had been prepared and we were officially ready to begin.

Everything was going according to plan, until we got to the observance of the very small cup of "homemade wine". The right scripture had been read, the unleavened bread had been discussed and eaten, and we were all set for the finale: the cup that represented the Blood of Christ. I stood there as leader and pastor of the church, the man conducting this very special ceremony. I held up the tiny cup, we prayed and blessed it, and the congregation drank.

I'm telling you, when I drank that homemade wine it went down my throat like a volcano. I swear it must have been 100 proof. I could feel my face turning red as I struggled to get it down and keep my composure. I wanted to kick my right leg up and down and give out a big "Whoa!" after tasting what was in that small, sweet, innocent communion cup.

> *I swear it must have been 100 proof.*

If you had been at the church on this day, you would have heard one side of the church coughing and gasping as they tasted the tiny cup of wine. On the other side of the church, you could have heard the other half of the congregation saying, "Yum!"

I know that the day that Christ shed His blood was so very serious, and I am thankful for His redeeming sacrifice for all who believe in Him. I would never remove the weight and the importance of what Jesus did for us that day on Calvary. I would like to say that sometimes we take ourselves too seriously. I have met religious people that are so Heavenly minded that they do no earthly good.

I think this communion episode was a wakeup call to me. We can never recreate any religious event, no matter how holy we attempt to make it out to be, to become a substitute for the finished work of the Cross. When I read about Jesus, He was on earth doing His Father's business. He was around people who needed Him. Jesus came to people whose lives were in shambles, who had short comings and who had made bad choices. Jesus was a friend to the people that religious people would not befriend.

To swallow my holy religious piousness and kick my leg a little was a way for me to laugh at any attempt to make my doings "holier than thou". I want to be around people that I can help in their walk with the Lord. I want to be able to point others to the true communion. Jesus never shied away from being with people that religion would have otherwise rejected. I have met some people under steeples that really could use a shot of Big Momma's brew.

ONE FOOT IN THE GRAVE

It was one of those typical fall mornings, the air was almost wet and the leaves were shades past their illuminating fall colors. It wasn't high noon, but it wasn't early morning either. My phone rang; the voice on the other end said they needed help, and they needed it quickly.

I pastor a church in north Georgia on the southern side of our city. When you pastor, you get to meet many people in your community that may never attend your church. I am a very outgoing person. That God-given character trait is probably one of my best qualities and it may be why the Lord has called me into the ministry. Our congregation is a small but tight-knit group of people. When you pastor people who you regularly associate with, you sometimes are called to care for the needs of family members you have never met before.

I feel like those small church congregations are very valuable to the well-being of the soul of their communities: those aforementioned tight-knit groups that take care of one another. Sometimes the smaller church groups are intimidated by the larger churches with big television programs and big building projects. Those big assemblies need big money and big support. Don't get me wrong, I thank God for the large churches just like I thank God for all of our ministries. Everyone is needed.

One year, I was called out on Christmas Eve late at night to pray with and talk to a man who I had never met. This gentleman had terminal cancer and hadn't slept in days. Fear had gripped him so tightly that he would not eat, sleep, or turn off a light. I was with my family on Christmas Eve and one of his daughters knew my name and called my phone and asked if I would come over to pray.

I'm telling you that the power of God is with us when we say yes, even in the most inconvenient of times. I drove over to the place where he lived and made my way inside the home to meet this man. I spoke to him for a bit, and then I prayed with him. As I prayed with him you could actually see his fear leave that house. They told me that after I left he got up out of his recliner, turned the television off, turned off all the lights, then went to bed and slept through the night.

Back to the original phone call. On this particular day when my cell phone rang, it was a local funeral home. They had a crisis. A family was laying a loved one to rest at a nearby cemetery and the minister that was in charge had gotten into an accident and was taken to the hospital. The funeral home director thought of me since my church was close by. I just happened to be at the church and could be at the gravesite in twenty minutes. I believe in having a proper burial, so I rushed to get to the location. Keep in mind that I knew nothing about the deceased or the family.

When I reached the cemetery, the family and friends were all standing by the graveside waiting on a minister. They all had on funeral attire: the typical suits and ties. The pallbearers were dressed in white shirts with black ties under their black suit jackets. The funeral home had their tent with their name on it at the site, and the provided chairs where lined up under the tent for the immediate family to sit in. They were all waiting on me.

I pulled through the small drive of the cemetery around the long line of cars, all the way up to the hearse. The funeral home director met me and gently pointed with his out stretched arm towards the family, who were all obviously stricken with sorrow. I made my way up the little path with my tie blowing in the wind and my Bible under my arm. As I made my way towards the family, I was looking hastily to the location where I was to conduct the ceremony. It is customary to stand at the head of the deceased and pay the last respects at the gravesite. After shaking a few hands, with apologies for the loss to those immediate family members under the tent, I maneuvered around the people to find my place to stand. Then it happened: I stepped in a hole right there under the tent. It wasn't a huge hole, but it was big enough to break a leg in.

I thought to myself that it could have been a lot worse, I could have tripped and knocked over the coffin. I started looking around for the coffin, and for the deceased person. It was then that I noticed a small box sitting on a table. Yes, that's right—this person had been cremated and was going to be buried in that hole. I had just stepped in a grave! That was a first!

This story is always humorous when I retell it. You have probably heard that old adage about having one foot in the grave. Well, I can actually say that happened to me. Thank God that it was not deep and that I reacted and stepped out of the hole quickly.

Some people live their lives with one foot in the grave. They are always dying. Have you ever been around people that are always sick and going to the doctor or just complaining about their health? I have. I am a firm believer that you get what you speak of. I don't want to speak illness and disease on myself. I love life and I look forward to the next day while still enjoying living in the present day. Outside of that faithful day, you would be hard pressed to find me with one foot in the grave. I'm a very positive person. I'm upbeat and I'm always looking for and hoping for the best.

> *Some people live their lives with one foot in the grave.*

Will there be days that are not as good as other days? Of course. But keeping a positive outlook and speaking good things is a much better way to attract better things in your life. I have chosen not to look for sickness and poverty in my life.

When I was a young boy, around the age of ten or twelve, my dad and I would go rabbit hunting. As a young boy, I would walk through the brush and thick woods very timidly. I would start lagging behind and my dad would ask me why I wasn't keeping up. I was looking for snakes and I did not want to step on one. My dad would tell me that we were not snake hunting.

If you are looking for snakes, you will find one. I am not looking for sickness. I am not looking for poverty. When you start looking for things that will bring you down and destroy you, you already have one foot in the grave.

What's That Sound beneath My Feet

I have a very good friend in Atlanta who pastors a very large church. His name is Bishop Dale Bronner. He is one of the classiest people I know and operates everything with a spirit of excellence. I first met Bishop Bronner at a ministers' meeting in Tennessee. We were staying in the same hotel and we spoke in the lobby for quite some time. He told me about his church and where it was located in Atlanta and said for me to come by when I had the opportunity. Bishop Bronner is always dressed to impress. I always tell him that I can imagine him working out in the gym or on a treadmill in a three piece suit. He is so clean!

He has midweek service on Thursday night, which is very unusual in the south. But, that makes it convenient for pastors like me to attend. I visited on a few different occasions; his teaching is life changing. Bishop Bronner has an extensive vocabulary. He could speak for twenty minutes and I may not even comprehend what was spoken if he didn't break it down for me. I always tell his congregation that the difference between Bishop Bronner and myself is that the words that he speaks already have a definition and the words that I speak are a combination of two or three words mixed together, that may or may not have a real definition.

I remember attending a meeting on a Thursday night. It was a dark time for me; my dad was fighting cancer and it was getting the best of him. I had gotten to the church early and prayer was taking place. I felt someone behind me tap me on the shoulder. Her name was Mrs. White, and she gave me one hundred dollars. I did not need any money, so why did she give this to me? She looked at me right in the eye and said that the Holy Spirit wanted her to give it to me. I took comfort that the Lord saw me and her approaching me was a sign that He was with me.

I try to attend a Thursday meeting at Bishop's church at least three times a year. One time after the service, I was shaking Bishop's hand and telling him how much I loved the message. He asked me to preach for him the next week.

"Wow, what an honor!" I thought. He has around twenty thousand members and he trusts me to stand in his stead. I remember him telling me to have fun and not be nervous, just allow the Lord to use you. I have ministered on several occasions since that time, and it always is an honor that I do not take lightly.

Let me describe for you what it is like being the guest speaker at Word of Faith. When you pull up in the parking lot, a staff member will be waiting for you and will direct you to a special place marked for a guest speaker to park. They will open the door for you and carry any and all materials you may need carried. You are escorted to the door where another staff member welcomes you and then carries you down a long hallway to an elevator. The elevator takes you to another floor where you are escorted to a hospitality room. In that room, which is decorated with the finest chairs, sofas, paintings money can buy, there is food and fruit and juice and anything else one could possibly want or need. The people at Word of Faith taught me the spirit of excellence in greeting guests!

When Bishop asks me to minister, I step up my game to the highest level that I possibly can. I wear my best suit—freshly dry cleaned—and I make sure my shirt is heavily starched. It takes me about an hour and a half to drive from my house to the church in Atlanta. On this particular speaking engagement, I had left home early to run a few errands in the Atlanta area. I was completing my first few tasks when I started hearing a noise that I wasn't familiar with. After two or three times of running in and out of different locations, I kept hearing that same noise, and it kept getting louder. I was looking up in the sky, under the car, and even at other people and yet I could not pin point where the noise was coming from or exactly what the noise was.

After I completed my errands, I still had about forty minutes of free time. I decided to go to a men's clothing store that I like to visit when I am in the area. I was walking around in that store with my thoughts on the evening service and the delight of being asked to minister, and I was still hearing that same noise. "Click clack, click clack"... what was that? Oh no, I had stepped in chewing gum!

> "Click clack, click clack"... what was that?

I walked out of the store to take a closer look. Lo and behold, it wasn't gum at all. My shoe was coming apart! The whole sole of my shoes was coming off of the shoe itself. What if I had been at Word of Faith? What if I had been walking across the stage with everyone watching? Oh my goodness, I would have been so embarrassed. Thank God I was at a clothing store. I purchased a pair of shoes and left with a thankful heart.

Sometimes in life we can find ourselves in some very precarious positions. There will be times that you want to escape and not know how. You can find yourself in embarrassing moments and wonder how to handle them exactly. I like the passage of scripture that says that when those moments come, a way of escape is made. When I feel those unpleasant seasons come, I ask the Lord to show me the way. He said He would not put more on us than we can handle. He knew I would not be able to handle walking across that stage without my sole.

> "There is no shame in my game."

There is a saying in the world, "There is no shame in my game." I know from life experiences that this is simply not true. No one I have ever met wants to purposefully do something or say something that would embarrass them. The biggest fear of any teenager is putting themselves in a position where they can be embarrassed. They are deathly afraid of falling down, having food stuck between their teeth, entering the wrong class, or having a big pimple on their nose. Anyone reading this can recall a moment that you really wished had not happened.

When we get embarrassed, the first thing we want to do is pretend like we are not. If we fall down, we jump up quickly and act as if it did not happen. The strange thing about being embarrassed is that although we may try to hide it, everyone knows we are embarrassed. People can tell by the look on your face. They tell you that your face is turning red in an attempt to embarrass you further. When we experience shame, our blood rushes to the surface to try and cover our shame. It never works, it only exposes our shame more. The blood of Jesus is the only blood that can cover our shame!

If you desire to walk through this life without shame, get your soul reborn so your walk will not be exposed. Jesus can give you a brand new walk and you can walk across the stage of life knowing that He has covered your shame.

Meeting Mickey

Chloe was four years old and she was my only child. I have always wanted to show my daughter new adventures. We had planned a trip to Orlando, Florida and that place that gets a whole lot of money from all over the world. It was our first ever trip to Disney and the Magic Kingdom. We were all Disney rookies, so we fit right in with the crowd. Going on a Disney vacation is no small feat—and it isn't cheap either. I remember standing in line to enter the park on our first day. The man in front of me purchased four tickets to four theme parks and the teller said it would be $1000. They had not seen one single thing or ridden one single ride and had already dropped a thousand dollars.

We flew from Atlanta to the Orlando International Airport. It was Chloe's first time flying. She was so cute with her little suit case walking through the terminal. On the plane, we sat her beside the window so she could better capture the flying experience. She got in her seat and closed the window shade. It wasn't that she didn't want to look out, my daughter has never cared about bright sunshine because it always makes her squint. If I recall correctly, the most she got out of the plane ride was the tray that you can let down on the back of the seat in front of you. She noticed that when your tray was down, they served you snacks.

Children, for the most part, can't distinguish between distances and times. When we landed and got a cab to carry us to our resort, Chloe kept asking where our car was. It did not register to her that we had been traveling at five hundred miles an hour for nearly two hours. We were a long way away from our vehicle.

We made it into the Magic Kingdom. If anyone knows how to do vacation, it is Disney! There we were on Main Street with the castle in the background. It was more overwhelming to my wife and me than it was for Chloe. We had grown up watching the black and white Disney movies and seeing Tinkerbelle fly around the castle with her glittering wand. The sights and sounds were just as we imagined: bright colors, smiling faces, singing and dancing—the smell of happiness was in the air. This was going to be great!

We saw Space Mountain with its long lines. Space Mountain is an indoor roller coaster that makes you feel as if you are traveling through space. We went to Tomorrow Land and rode several rides, including The Carousel of Life. We rode the submarine ride that goes under the water. We rode the Little Mermaid ride that takes you through the story of the Little Mermaid. We went through the Swiss Family Robinson adventure. Yes, we rode the "It's a Small World" ride. Anyone who has ever ridden that ride knows that you will be singing that theme song for the rest of the day!

We ate lunch and had refreshing snacks like a Mickey ice cream with the big ears. We drank sodas with a Mickey straw, but we still had not seen Mickey. Today when you go to Disney, the characters are all over the park. They are walking around on the streets and at different locations to greet the visitors. On our first trip there, all of the characters were in Mickey's Toon Town. We had to get on a train that runs around the kingdom to reach our destination.

When we walked into that area, we started seeing different characters and we knew we were in the right place. Winnie the Pooh and Tigger met us with arms wide open. We got to meet Pluto and Donald Duck and even get their autographs. We stood in line to meet Snow White and Sleeping Beauty. We even got to hug and take pictures with Goofy and Daisy Duck. We knew we were getting close when we came across Minnie Mouse. It was so sweet: Chloe ran over and hugged Minnie like she was her best friend. But we had come to see the star of the show…Mickey.

The set up was a house that was designed as if it was Mickey's own house. You could stand in line with all the other boys and girls and parents and grandparents to meet Mickey. You could take a journey while in line and see Mickey's house. We went through the living room and saw his couch and chair and television. There were pictures of Mickey and Minnie hanging on the wall to make it feel like home. The line carried you through Mickey's kitchen where you saw a table with cheese on it. Then, you went down the hall to Mickey's' bedroom. Mickey's slippers were on the floor and all the other costumes that we are used to seeing him wear were hanging in his closet.

We were getting so close to Mickey that we could hear the other children talking to him. Then we were next! It was our time! All the money, the strain of travel, the long lines, the sweat of summer, and everything that goes with taking a vacation like this was all about to pay off. It was all about my baby girl and her having the best summer vacation ever!

The attendant motioned for us to come on in. I still remember it like it was yesterday— although it has been over twenty years ago. We rounded the corner and there was Mickey: the Big Guy, the main star, big mouse on campus. Carol and I momentarily forgot that we had brought our little girl with us as we pushed her to the side and ran into Mickey's arms. It was great! Our childhood hero was right there!

Then we came to our senses and Chloe had her time with Mickey. Our daughter has always been tenderhearted. She hugged Mickey and she cried with joy. It was all worth every bit of it! I would say that I would do it all over again, but we have over and over again. Today we are carrying our grandson on the same adventure.

There are many times in life when we think we are doing something for others and we find out that it was more rewarding for us. We give out turkeys every year for Thanksgiving from our church and every year on the surface it seems like we are being a blessing to others when it fact we are the ones who walk away feeling blessed. It says in the Good Book that it is more blessed to give than to receive. You know that is really true. When we carried our daughter to see that rat, little did I know how emotional it would be for both my wife and me. It was a true blessing.

> There are many times in life when we think we are doing something for others and we find out that it was more rewarding for us.

Take the time and effort to use your energy and resources for others. It may be for your spouse, your children, your family, a neighbor, a co-worker, or even a stranger. When you sacrifice, you will be the one who is blessed. Reach outside of yourself and do for others. You won't regret it.

Welcome to the Family

My wife and I have been married for twenty nine years and it has been absolutely wonderful. When I hear that couples are having trouble in their marriage, it is just difficult for me to comprehend. When people have issues deep enough to consider divorce, it sounds so foreign to me. Don't get me wrong, we are not immune to problems. But, I just can't see my life being any better without my wife in it. Do we always see eye to eye? Of course not. Have we ever had heated disagreements? You dang tootin'! When I signed up, I signed up for the long haul.

I remember when we first met. I was driving through a parking lot and she was walking to her car. We struck up a conversation which eventually led to her getting in my car to go to a party hosted by one of her friends. We had been acquainted with each other prior to this first time being together. Carol was working with a girl that I had dated a few times and I had tried to fix Carol up with my friend John. They did not work out and there was no chemistry on my end with Carol's coworker either. The night we got together, the stars were aligned.

We dated for a total of about six months and got married on October 31. Yep, on Halloween! We did not necessarily choose that date; it was the only weekend we both had off work together. We drove to Sevierville, Tennessee to get it done. As we were filling out the licenses, we signed the date and just looked at each other and laughed. What a day to get married!

When you marry someone, you are not only marrying an individual, you are connecting with an entire family. Carol has two brothers and two sisters and I only have one sister. Both of my parents were alive when we married, but Carol's father Charlie was deceased. My immediate family may appear very small but I grew up with large family get-togethers on Christmas and other holidays. We both have nieces and nephews and brothers and sisters-n-law.

I remember my first Christmas with Carol's family. You know every family has some unique thing they do when they get together. Some families draw names and exchange gifts, some purchase gift for everyone, some just celebrate for the children, while others may just recognize the patriarchs or matriarchs of the family. In Carol's family they do something that I wasn't used to and had never seen before. They all sit around the largest room in the house. People are on the floor, sitting in each other's laps, or sitting on folding chairs, but each person is sitting in a way to see one another.

Now, my family get together can best be described as a mad house. We have so many young children and all they want is to get to the gifts. Carol's mom Annie Dell lived on a fixed income, but she would always see to it that everyone received something at Christmas. I was just an observer, not knowing exactly what was taking place. Sometimes when I am in unfamiliar territory, I have learned to sit back and not make any sudden movements, but rather watch others and follow their lead. While we were all sitting in the best circle we could, each person would go around the room and open a gift from someone. Each person would open a gift while others looked on. Now, Annie Dell had gotten everyone a card for Christmas. Each person would open their card and read it.

As I am observing the Christmas tradition and my new wife's family, I notice that when each person opened their card from Carol's mother, there was a five dollar bill inside. I thought to myself that these people don't know me that well and I don't know them that well. So, what better time to introduce myself. I have never been one to hold back when it comes to having a little fun. Humor and laughter is the best to break any ice and bring commonality to strangers.

Where the idea came from, I don't know. But, I'm sure glad it came. I reached into my wallet while no one was watching and took out a twenty dollar bill. When it was my time to open the card from my mother-in-law, I played it to the hilt. I could have won a Grammy for this performance.

Every eye was on me; the stage was set. Each person had opened their card and read a generic Merry Christmas greeting and thanked Annie Dell for the five dollars. They all sat there as I slowly opened my card a little higher up so all would take notice. When I opened the card, that twenty dollar bill fell out onto the floor. That got their attention.

I was able to summon some fake some tears as I started to read this "welcome to the family" message that I had fabricated from Carol's mom. I gave this huge thank you to my mother-in-law for such a welcome into the family. By this time, no one was listening to my made up welcome to the family, they were all wondering why I got twenty dollars and they just got five dollars. Heck, Annie Dell was wondering the same thing. After I explained that I had slipped my own money into the card, we all had a big laugh.

> *Things in life are not always as they always appear.*

Things in life are not always as they always appear. Check the room, and check for clowns.

Embrace the traditions of others. Laugh and enjoy the creativity around you and the creativity in you. One day the family circle will be broken, so sit in it while you can.

THE NAP

I am always asking people where there are from. When I am asked this question, people are typically referring to my southern accent. Usually people ask me if I am from Louisiana; they think I have a Cajun accent. That is always strange to me because I am just an old Georgia boy. I have recently gotten used to people saying it, so I surmise that there must be some truth to my Cajun sound. The closest I can come to knowing anyone from Louisiana is watching that gator show on television, although I can honestly say that I haven't seen one episode in its entirety.

Cultures and customs from all over the world, and even from our own country, are fascinating to me. Down in the south, we refer to any kind of soda as a Coke. When we ask you if you would like a coke, we could be offering a variety of different carbonated beverages. People I have met from the northern part of the United States refer to soda as pop. I we could discuss many more synonymous terms for things that northerners and southerners use in greater detail, but I will refrain.

I guess you can imagine when my friend Bishop Joseph comes from Zambia to stay with us in Georgia that there is plenty of miscommunication. One time when his wife Grace was with us, a lady in our church asked her if the women in Zambia wore pants. Grace was appalled. Why would an American woman ask if women in Zambia wore panties? Pants in their native language refers to the under garments. What we would call pants in America, they call trousers. It is funny now, but at the time Grace was very much caught off guard.

That example of miscommunication leads me to the first time Joseph came to stay with us in Georgia. Joseph is from Zambia. The first time he came to stay with us and witness firsthand all of our cultural differences was definitely eye opening for him. When we picked him up at the airport and were driving the hour and a half trip home from Atlanta, Joseph was looking out the window into the sky with a puzzled look on his face.

"Do those things...those twister things...just fall out of the sky?" he asked with an almost perceptible quiver in his voice. He was asking us about tornadoes. He had heard about them in the news from America and how they can kill and cause such damage. We laughed at his question because it was a sunny day with very few clouds in the sky. Joseph did not know whether or not a tornado could pop out of the clear blue sky, so we did what we could to calm his fears.

Next, Joseph asked us if those big and tall...then he stopped talking, paused in thought, and began gesturing with his hands in the air and making a deep, growling noise. He asked, "Do they come into your home?" After some questioning, we figured out that he was asking about grizzly bears.

"Do grizzly bears come to your home?" Joseph asked with a quivering voice, much like he had for his question about the tornados. We laughed again. He had heard stories were people were mauled and killed by bears and he wanted to be on guard while in Georgia. So, you can already see many cultural differences already coming into play.

The journey from Zambia is very long, and jet lag can take a toll on a person when traveling such a great distance through numerous time zones changes. Zambia is six to seven hours ahead of our time zone. My wife had prepared a room for Joseph and had given him extra blankets, a candy dish, and just about any other personal items he may have needed while on his visit. Joseph arrived on a Saturday. He was to be our guest speaker at the church Sunday.

All went according to plan. We settled in on Saturday and got some rest, and then we went about our business on Sunday morning. Joseph is a powerful speaker and has witnessed God do mighty miracles. Recounting some of those miracles was the basis of his message at church, and it seemed as if everyone in the audience was moved by his stories. After church, we grabbed a quick lunch and returned to our home.

When we got home from church on that Sunday afternoon, my wife told Joseph that we would take a nap and resume our afternoon activities later. My wife can lie down and take a nap most Sunday afternoons, but napping has never been in my skill set. After a couple of hours had gone by, Carol asked if she should start dinner. I said that it was a good idea since we only had eaten a small lunch and hadn't eaten any breakfast. My wife is a great cook. She prepared a great big dinner for our guest: way more than she would have prepared if it had been just us two.

A few hours went by and there was no sign of movement from Joseph's room. He must have been napping very well. Then it got dark. Evening was rolling in and it was getting later and later, but there was still no sign of Joseph. We did not want to disturb him because we know how grueling those long flights can be. It eventually became so late that Carol just fixed a plate and wrapped it up with plastic wrap and left it out for Joseph if he should awaken in the night. My wife and I went on to bed and slept through the night.

The Nap

Carol and I got up the next morning at the usual time and were drinking our morning coffee when we heard the door to Joseph's room open. He came down the hall to where we were drinking coffee and politely asked us, "So this nap...how long do we nap?"

Joseph did not know what a nap was in his language. Carol later told me that he must have gotten very hungry in his room because he had eaten every single piece of candy in the candy dish. We can laugh about it now, but it really taught us a lesson. We may live in a modern world and can easily travel to any location in the world, but we are also divided by our cultures.

Have you ever been misunderstood? Have you ever misunderstood someone else? I meet people all the time that are at odds with other people for some reason or another. I always wonder if it is all because of a miscommunication or a break down in what was really meant. The bad thing about communication is that sometimes we assume in our minds the meaning or motivation behind what someone tells us. Instead of actually asking the person what they meant, we will run it through our minds over and over again and play the conversation in our head like a record on repeat. We can misinterpret something and then let it eat at

> *Have you ever been misunderstood? Have you ever misunderstood someone else?*

us for a very long time. Relationships are broken because of misunderstandings. Brothers and sisters can get into hostile relations because of something that was taken the wrong way.

Are you at odds today with someone? Can you even remember what it was that built the wall between you? Ask yourself if you could have misunderstood them, or perhaps have been misunderstood? Life is entirely too short to be feuding with other people. Slow down and think about it. Take a Nap!

I DON'T EVEN KNOW THAT MAN THAT WELL

It was that the time of year when summer was coming to a close. My wife loves the sunshine. With the dread of winter approaching, Carol asked me if we could plan a trip to the beach for one last summer vacation. If my wife wants something and I have the ability to make it happen, it's going to happen. We live in north Georgia and most of our friends and neighbors travel to Panama City beach if they want some beach time. Panama City Beach is about a six hour drive from our house and very convenient. The down sides for us at Panama City Beach are that we have been so many times and the cost of vacationing there has risen drastically over the years. I always like trying new things and having new experiences.

I decided to check on the economics of a trip to Miami. After doing some investigating, we discovered that it did not cost much more for us to fly to Miami than it would for us to drive to Panama City Beach. Since we had never been to Miami, we decided that would be how we would spend our end of summer vacation.

We flew out of Atlanta on a Sunday afternoon, which ended up being a very bumpy ride. During the flight we hit some turbulence due to the heat over the Everglades. At one point, I looked over at Carol and witnessed her trying to catch her coffee which had gone a good two feet in the air. I heard someone say once that God had allowed man to discover flight to guarantee that he would pray. On this flight I knew that truer words has never been spoken. It was very frightening. We did manage to land safely in Miami. Thank the Lord the flight home was without incident.

Our plan was to fly Miami and then take a taxi to the Trump Resort and just enjoy the beach. We made no plans to travel around the area, only to relax at the resort. I would like to add here that the resort was top notch. We were really glad we chose to stay there. Our room was second to none and the restaurants in the resort are top shelf. The staff at Trump Resort was also very welcoming and they assisted us with any need we had.

The view from our room was majestic. Blue skies, a few white clouds, plenty of sunshine, turquoise water, and a gentle breeze made for a great three days on the beach to end our summer. Being with the woman I love made it just that much sweeter.

Carol and I enjoy just sitting and relaxing. We tend to start days off with coffee and some inspirational reading and prayer time. Sitting on the balcony during our normal routine just added to a perfect day. After a few hours of sitting and drinking our morning coffee, we started our day on the beach. The weather was fantastic and the water was beautiful. The whole setting was magnificent.

We don't do what would be considered a lot of swimming, but we do like to sunbathe. After getting extra crispy in the hot sun, we like to cool off in the ocean or pool. Let me be clear, my wife is the one that embraces the sun's rays. I, on the other hand, spend the majority of my beach time under an umbrella. Carol can walk by a light bulb and get a tan. I usually just look like a lobster. That's just how we roll.

It was our first day on the beach, and it was nice. I made my way out to the ocean while Carol was reading her book. I was standing in about chest deep water enjoying the array of fish swimming between my legs and nipping at my ankles. The water was so clear that I could clearly see the different colors and sizes of fish. I enjoy seeing wild life in its natural habitat. I must confess: I hate those little suckers hitting my feet and legs. I bet if those fish wrote a book, they would say how much they hate seeing guys like me in their water.

On this day, there was a man standing beside me just a few yards away. He was an older gentleman with a long sleeve shirt, a big brimmed hat, and oversized sunglasses. I never meet a stranger. So, I started up a conversation with him. Just to make small talk, I commented on how beautiful it was out there. He responded with some language I had never heard before.

In Miami, people come from everywhere: South America, Germany, Russia, Mexico, Canada, and even Georgia. I am not sure where this man was from, and I am pretty sure that he did not have a clue what I was saying or where I was from either. After a few facial expressions and hand gestures, I concluded that it was great just being on the beach!

That evening my wife and I went to an Argentinean steak house. It was the best meal I had had in a long time. We both ordered steak and mashed potatoes; it was simple but it was delicious. We spent a quiet evening out and returned to our room only to repeat the process again the next day.

This is where vacation got interesting. It started like any other day: coffee, a little meditation and reading, and then off to the beach. It was about midday of the second day of our Miami trip. Carol and I both were out in the water just taking in all the

I Don't Even Know That Man That Well

scenery. Then Carol said, "Hey! There is your friend from yesterday" as she pointed behind us a little farther out in the water. Sure enough, it was him. He had on the same long sleeves, big hat and sunglasses as before, so there was no mistaking him.

My wife said, "Joey. I think he is in trouble." I looked over and sure enough, he was a little too far out for his or my comfort. I started swimming towards him and I raised my voice to ask if he was alright. He waived his hand and I heard, "Yaaaa." To me, that meant that he was just fine, so I started swimming back to Carol.

I soon learned, however, that "Yaaaa" evidently means, "My butt is drowning. Can you help me?"

Carol said, "Joey, I really think he is in trouble." I turned and looked back at him. By that time, his hat was sideways, his glasses had slid off, and his head was bobbing up and down in the water. I immediately turned and started swimming towards him.

Our minds are truly awesome. It's amazing just how many thoughts we can have in one split second. The man was approximately twenty yards away from me. As I was swimming towards him, thoughts ran through my mind like lightning bolts:

1. People who are drowning usually panic and drown the person trying to rescue them.

2. I did not want to go out like this.

3. He looked like, by his age and appearance, he has lived a pretty long life.
4. I still got stuff to do.
5. I don't even know him that well!

It sounds kind of funny saying this now, but it was reality at that moment. Thank God that several other guys had made their way over to where we were thrashing about. We calmed the man down as best we could. Someone rode up on a jet ski with a rope and someone else arrived on a paddle board. We hoisted him up on the paddle board and made our way to the shore. By this time his wife and friends were on the beach receiving him with joy and sweet relief. Long story short, he lived to see another day.

How many people around us are treading the waters of life and are about to go under? How many are crying out for help? How often do we just dismiss someone who is in trouble because we cannot understand their language? Every one of us will try to hide our personal struggles when we are dealing with life's issues. We wear masks to cover up our anguish and worry. We speak in ways that sound like everything is alright, but in reality we are going under.

Speak up! Find yourself a friend that you can connect with: a real friend who you can tell anything to and who won't judge you. In our society that lives off of social media, everyone comes across like they have hundreds of friends. That's fake news! In life, we are very blessed if we have one or two friends that we can confide in. I know that there are exceptions, but from my experience the numbers are very low.

We all have family members, neighbors, co-workers, and acquaintances in our lives that are in trouble and we cannot understand their language. I would challenge you to become more receptive to those around you. I believe in vibes and signals. Even though I could not speak this man's language, his body language shouted "I am drowning! Help!"

There are people all around us being swallowed up with the everyday problems of this world. They are crying out for help. You could be in the water just deep enough and close enough to help someone out of real trouble.

> They are crying out for help.

THAT'S A BIG SPIDER ON THE WALL

This is another tale from our Zambian travels. On this particular trip, it was my wife and daughter's first trip to Africa. I love being with my friends in Zambia. I have tried to make it a habit of going there every other year. If the journey was not so difficult, I would go there more often. They love us when we are arriving. They always receive us such with a warm reception at the airport with cheers and flowers and singing; it is like nothing else I've seen. Joseph (you'll remember him from previous stories) and his wife Grace welcome us and host us in their home.

I think years ago people would travel to different regions, even in the United States, and stay with relatives and friends instead of hotels. That is a thing of the past for most people, which is probably why there are a dozen hotels on every interstate exit. When

Joseph and Grace come to America, they stay with us in our home. We do not host other people in our home, not because we wouldn't, but it just has not been our practice. When you host others in your home, everyone is inconvenienced. My daughter gives up her bedroom when Joseph is with us. Chloe has to sleep in another room, and which means moving clothes and makeup and shoes…and more shoes. We make room in the closet for our guests, and that requires moving whatever Chloe thinks she may for the duration of their stay.

It is no different when we stay in Zambia with Joseph. They move their sons around, and they may sleep on the floor or at some friend's home. They make big sacrifices for us and we appreciate it so much. When you have guests in your home for a few days, you don't act the same or dress the same as when it is just you and your close family. Well, let me just say, our personal home relaxing attire is a little more appropriate when guests are over than it is when we are home alone. I'll let you paint that picture in your head.

On this particular trip, we were sleeping in an upstairs bedroom. Off to the side of it, we had an extra bathroom. I believe it was the only room upstairs. There was a big mattress that sat on the floor and all three of us slept on it. If you know anything about how I sleep, one big mattress is not sufficient for me by myself. I toss and turn throughout the night. My wife

That's a Big Spider on the Wall

says I have "flip and flop syndrome." It's kind of like restless leg syndrome, but my entire body is restless and basically tosses and turns all night. So, all three of us sleeping together was a challenge.

After being with them for a day or so, the jet lag wore off and we began to get settled in. I remember it like it was yesterday: Carol, Chloe, and I were sitting in the family room on the sofa. Joseph was somewhere else in the house and Grace was preparing a meal for us. Then I felt this hand pinch me tightly. I turned toward Carol and Chloe was gasping.

"What is it? What's wrong?" I asked with a worried tone in my voice.

You should have seen the spider going up the wall across the room. I swear that thing was bigger than my hand. I wore no less than a size nine running shoe. My mind told me it was a tarantula. To this day, I do not know what kind of spider it was, but it was the biggest spider that I had ever seen. I was pretty certain that it wasn't their pet. I was sure, however, that it was the most deadly South African spider ever!

My wife was urging me to do something. So, I yelled for Joseph. Joseph came in the room and asked what the problem was. I told him about the huge spider and I asked him how he was going to kill it.

Joseph let out this larger than life laugh. His laugh is so memorable; he can laugh and it echoes around the house. Joseph said, "In Zambia, we don't kill the spider because the spider kills and eats the mosquitoes." My response was that in America, we kill spiders, mosquitoes, and any other creepy crawly thing.

> There was a huge spider in that house, and he probably wasn't alone!

Can you imagine how the remainder of the trip was for the three of us in the upstairs bedroom? One of us would sleep while the other two sat back to back on the floor keeping watch. There was a huge spider in that house, and he probably wasn't alone!

We survived our stay and had no other encounters with that prehistoric creature. Isn't it amazing that we could not sleep for fear and the very thing we were afraid of did not disturb Joseph and his family. Everyone deals with some type of fear: fear of heights, fear of gaining weight, fear of snakes, fear of the dark, fear of dying, and so on. Fear is something that happens to everyone, and it is something that we internalize. When I say that fear is something we internalize, I am referring to how and what we allow our mind think. The fear factor is what we think about something that causes fear.

Some people say that you need to "face your fear and overcome it." They will jump out of airplanes, eat exotic foods, and do other dare-devilish things to face their fears. I have read that we have not been given

That's a Big Spider on the Wall

the spirit of fear. If my Creator did not give me fear and I began to experience it, I need to do something to get rid of it.

One time, the disciples where on a boat in the middle of a storm. They were afraid they were going to die. Jesus happened to be on the same boat and in the same storm, but He was sleeping soundly. How could He sleep in the same conditions that the disciples were so fearful in? The answer is peace. Jesus is the peace speaker, He is the one who can calm the storm and cause peace to come in our most frightening moments.

How could Joseph and his family sleep while we were afraid in the same house? Maybe because they knew that spider; maybe they had gotten used to that environment. Maybe that spider wasn't as big as we remember it being. Maybe they knew it wasn't harmful. I think it is the peace of God that passes all our understanding.

When fear comes in your mind, and it will, remember that is did not come from the Lord. Tell fear to leave you. Tell fear, "I am a child of the Most High, whom shall I fear!"

Think on things that are true, honest, and of a good report. Don't give fear a room in your thoughts or it will move in. You can have the rest and peace of God by just calling on the name of Jesus.

RED MEAT IN A BAG

This is another one of those Zambian stories. When I travel to Zambia, they are the most welcoming people that I have ever encountered in my travels. After hours and hours of air-travel, it is so refreshing to land in a little community call Chingola with such a warm welcome. The airport has been greatly improved over the years, but when I first started going to Chingola it was a much smaller airport.

Joseph and I met in 1997 in Atlanta. A large church with a world outreach program was hosting an international conference and they had sponsored Joseph and his wife Grace to come to the meetings. I was attending these meetings as well, and that is when we met for the first time. It was during one of the lunch break sessions; we met very briefly and exchanged addresses and phone numbers. This was before everyone had computers and cell phones. Some of our early communications were through letters. Letters—like when you take a writing utensil and write down on paper what you would like to say. Then when the letter is complete, you would have to travel to a post office where you would purchase a stamp. You always had to make sure the address was correct and the return address was in proper place. I know it sounds like it was so long ago, but I am old now. Joseph and I had written letters back and forth for a while when all of a sudden, he invited me to come to Zambia, Africa.

I started making arrangements to travel to Zambia and be with him within the year. My travel agent told me that he could get me tickets from Atlanta to London, then from London to Johannesburg, and finally from Johannesburg to Lusaka, Zambia. However, it was on Joseph to arrange for my travel once inside Zambia. Once I landed in Lusaka, I had to get on a smaller plane that seated around twenty passengers or so. It was one of those planes where you could see the pilot and co-pilot only a few feet from your seat.

In our letter writing, I confirmed that I would be arriving on a particular date. Joseph and I did make one or two phone calls to iron out some very important details. The dialect in Zambia is that of a British accent, which doesn't sound like anything this Georgia boy is accustomed to. I remember speaking on the phone through the international transfer. With the echo and the delay, it was difficult to catch everything he was saying. Joseph had told me that I would get on the small plane and it would carry me to Kitwe, Chingola, and Ndola. These were towns that I—nor anyone I knew—had ever heard of before. When I boarded the small aircraft, the pilot made the announcement of all the towns where we would be stopping. He named all that Joseph had mentioned and a few more in his dialect. Many thoughts raced through my mind– "What town was I suppose to get off in again? Where was Joseph going to meet me? Where was the nearest parachute? Would I even recognize Joseph when I saw him? After all, it had been a year or two since we had met. I finally decided that if I didn't see anyone I recognized when we landed, I would just stay on this little plane and then make my way back to Georgia!

We landed at the first town. The airport, if you could even call if that, was very small and had a dirt runway. I told the pilot that I wasn't sure if this was the correct town or not, and I asked him very politely not to leave until I checked it out. I got off the small plane and walked around the very small terminal. A couple of men were sitting outside; they did not even take notice of me, so I got back on the plane.

Then it all fell into place. We landed in Ndola, and I got off the plane just as I had before, and there was a great crowd gathered. They were singing so loud as a mass choir. As I approached, I could see Joseph and Grace: they greeted me with open arms. There were men to take my luggage and flowers brought to me with big welcoming banners for my arrival. Zambians are very warm people. My heart melts as I recall this love.

On another one of my journeys to Africa, my wife and daughter were able to accompany me. We were received with the same type of warm reception as I was the first time I landed in Ndola. On this particular trip, after a few days in Zambia they wanted to grant my family and I a special "bri." A bri is similar to a barbeque in America. During this special event, the women made one long line and the men stood in another line that was beside them. It took place was on a clear plain of what looked to be cleared off country side. There were little fires here and there in little fire pits about ten to twenty yards apart. The plan was that the women would fellowship together and the men would fellowship together around those open fires.

Since we were the special guests, we were placed front and center. I stood in front of the men's line and Carol and Chloe headed the women's line. When it was time for the celebration to begin, we walked forward and were handed a little see-through plastic bag. Inside the bag was a big piece of meat with the bloody juices moving around in the bottom of the bag. Well, as you can imagine, our imaginations ran wild. What was this? What animal did this come from? Was

Red Meat in a Bag

this monkey brains? What did this monkey do to make these folks mad?

I took my little bloody bag to my fire and began to cook it. I looked at my wife and daughter as they were led off to a separate fire with the women and our eyes me. Their eyes were actually screaming at me. We did not want to offend anyone by any means, so we just cooked our portion on the fire and followed the leadership of those wonderful people. The meat was actually very tasty. We never did find out what we ate that night. It may have been the best sirloin steak ever, so we may not ever want to find out exactly what was in that little bag.

On one occasion when Joseph and Grace came to visit us in Georgia, we had a church bon-fire. It was in late October when someone in the church wanted to host a church wide cookout on their property in the country. The night was cool and brisk; it was a great evening to sit around the fire and just fellowship. We had a great turn out from the church. People were so excited to spend time with Joseph and Grace in a casual setting.

One thing we love to do here around a fire in the south is to cook hotdog weenies on a stick over the fire. Each person gets a long stick and pokes it through a weenie on one end and holds it over the fire until it is cooked. I could see that our international guests had never done this before, so it was a new adventure for them. I could hear Grace asking Joseph what kind of meat is was and what part of the animal is was from. My reply was that I didn't know exactly what it was…we just call it a hotdog!

> We all live in the same world, but with so many different customs.

We all live in the same world, but with so many different customs. There are things that are familiar and unfamiliar to us. I embrace the variety of things around us. I really enjoy exposure to other cultures. One of the statements that I make often is, "Most of the people I know still live in a flat world."

Before men like Christopher Columbus began exploring our world, people were sure that their own personal corner of the world was all there was to see. We are so isolated from other cultures and yet we have all kinds of windows into other worlds. Men, women, boys, and girls from all over the world are not much different in their wants and their desires. It is our different cultures that shape us into having such different experiences.

I would encourage each of you to stretch yourself and your comfort zone by visiting new places and people. The world is so big and ready to be explored. There are new adventures waiting for you. You may find your next meal in a bag or on a stick! Go get it!

Magic Mic

There are many mega churches in the United States. A pastor friend of mine said that only about five percent of American Christians attend mega churches. Out of fifty-five million Christians in the States, only about five million attend a church that has a congregation of fifteen hundred to several thousand members. The remainder of the fifty million people attends churches all across America with roughly one hundred members or less. Saying that, more believers attend smaller churches that the large mega churches. That fact really highlights the importance of the smaller congregations.

My wife and I started our church several years ago from the ground up with just a handful of people to begin with. It was exciting, it was scary, and it was a lot of trial and error. I still remember when I found the little building we began our ministry in. In my early days speaking, and still sometimes even today, I used props and illustrations. I think it is important to do everything possible to make sure the people understand the message that is being presented. I have used golf clubs in sermons, I have made deviled eggs, I have used ladders, and I have even hurled an ax against the pulpit.

One day, I was riding around trying to find any location that we could rent or purchase to use for church service. Someone had told me about a man who had homes and buildings that he relocated from its current location to your property. I drove about thirty miles north to see if he had anything that we could use for a church building. I'm not sure that I can adequately explain this, but while I was driving I saw a chalkboard. It wasn't on the side of the road, mind you. I cannot clearly say if I had a vision or if the chalk board just appeared in my lucid daydream. My first thought was that I can use a chalkboard in my next sermon. I could draw out the fruits of Spirit on the chalkboard. Little did I know that I was about to have an encounter!

I found the lot with several buildings that could be relocated. When I got out of my truck, I saw lots of old homes, but one building stood out. There it was, sitting on crossties about five feet in the air with the side door hanging off of its hinges. I made my way to the open door and pulled myself up on my belly into the building. When I got inside, I found a chalkboard that went all the way down the wall. This building was used as a classroom at a local school. When I saw that chalkboard, chills went down my spine. The Spirit of the Lord was all over me. I knew that this was the one; it was perfect. Compared to the mega churches, this little building was not that much to look at. But as I recall, the leader of Christianity was not much to look at either.

Our new little sanctuary was small, but it was ours. After a few months in our new building, we started having five or six new families attend our church. It was fantastic and exciting. One of my cousins is married to a minister named Mike. I think it is always good to bring in different ministers to speak. I had asked Mike to come and speak on the following weekend. It was going to be our first time having a guest speaker. We firmly believe in hosting with a spirit of excellence. Being a new start up church with very little funding, we did what we could with what we had at the time. Our keyboard was on a saw horse made out of wood. Our one Sunday school room was a converted bathroom. I used a Radio Shack microphone. Some people use foam covers on their microphones. I never did like those covers because the sound was not as crisp and clear. When you use a cheap microphone, they tend to get dingy and rusty looking over time. They may work fine, but they look horrible.

As we were preparing for our guest speaker, we cleaned the bathrooms with extra care. We made sure the building had that freshly cleaned smell. The grass was freshly mowed and the shrubs had been trimmed.

Then my wife took notice of our dingy microphone. We tried to clean the mic, but it did not help. My quick-thinking wife had a great idea. She took what was called a permanent black marker and colored all of the rust on the microphone. It looked great.

Then it was time for our special guest speaker, Brother Michael. It was his first time speaking in our newly founded church. He started preaching, and it was intense. He was speaking straight from the heart. His aim was at the heart of the listener and his message was very compelling. While Brother Michael was speaking, he worked up a sweat like many passionate preachers often do. Right there in front of God and everybody, it started happening. That permanent marker was rubbing off from the top of microphone right and getting all over Brother Michael's chin.

The congregation went from paying close attention to the words being spoken to paying even closer attention to the transformation that was taking place. Were we really seeing what we were seeing? Was it the light that was casting a shadow on the speaker's face? Did he forget to shave his chin? It looked like he was growing a new beard right then and there.

When Brother Michael finished his sermon, he was calling for anyone who was willing to come and receive this life changing Savior, Jesus. The congregation was on the edge of their seats, but not because of the sermon. They were fascinated by the magic mic.

I got up as graciously as I could and told Brother Michael that I would close the sermon so he could go to the restroom. He gave me a puzzled look, and then hastened himself off the stage. We laugh today at that event, but it was really embarrassing for us and for Brother Michael.

Sometimes in life we can be found with egg on our face. The magic we had hoped for is nowhere to be found. When Jesus shed His blood, I am so thankful that it can be transferred from His body to our lives. We have all failed and done things we wish no one knew about. I am sure there are things we have been involved in that we would hope that the all-knowing God would not find out about. God is all-knowing and our lives cannot be hidden from Him. The only way to remove the stains in our lives is by the Blood of the Lamb. Brother Michael had to go and remove that marker from his face that day by washing with soap and water. The way we remove our stains is by washing with the blood. I have never heard that the blood is magic, but I am thankful that it is permanent!

> *Sometimes in life we can be found with egg on our face.*

AUTHOR CONTACT

To contact Pastor Joey Motes:

His Church
25 Adams Circle SE
Silver Creek, GA 30173
706-346-1627
Joeypastor7@aol.com
hischurchga.com